This journal belongs to:

_____

In loving memory of:

_____

ABOUT THE AUTHOR

Shaela Mauger and Harpermartin

Born and raised in Wagga Wagga regional New South Wales, Shaela has pursued her love of graphic design through university and began her career as a designer for a local printer.

Since becoming a mother, Shaela has fine tuned her passion for design towards what's most important to her: loved ones, and cherishing the time we have with them. Now, after half a decade of having her own design business, Shaela has launched Harpermartin — paying homage to her parents' family names — and this series of keepsake books, created to celebrate life and love in all its forms.

The series is available at www.harpermartin.com.au

Copyright © Shaela Mauger 2020

Cover image 'Silhouette of trees during night time' by Free Nature Stock on Pexels

All rights reserved. No part of this publication may be reproduced, stored in a retrieval system or transmitted, in any form or by any means, electronic, mechanical, photocopying, recording or otherwise, without prior permission of the copyright holder.

ISBN 978-0-6482778-8-0

MISSING YOU

In memory of my loved one

Table of Contents

All about my loved one... 3

All the things I love about you... 5

My favourite memories... 7,9

All the things I loved doing with you... 15-17

I miss you saying and doing... 19

You taught me... 21

I wish you were here for... 23

You would have loved this... 25

If you were here today I would tell you this... 27

A letter to you... 29-31

Stories people tell me about you... 33

All the things I remember about you now... 35

Drawings & Art 37-41

Pages to journal 43-49

Photo pages throughout

In memory of my Dad, Greg x

PREFACE

I'm so sorry someone you love has died. My Dad died when I was five years old so I understand what it feels like to miss someone you love.

This book is designed for you to write down everything you love and miss about your loved one. Stick in your favourite photos, write letters, draw pictures, do what brings you comfort.

Never compare your grief to others because everyone grieves differently. This person was a very special part of your life and they always will be. This journal helps you put down on paper all the feelings and memories you hold dear.

I am thinking of you!

With love,

Shaela xx
Founder, Harpermartin

All about my loved one...

Full name:

Nickname:

Date and place of birth:

The day you died:

Your favourite number:

Your favourite colour:

Your favourite team:

Your favourite hobby:

Your favourite saying:

Your nickname for me:

Photos

All the things I love about you...

Photos

My favourite memories...

Photos

My favourite memories…

Photos

Photos

Photos

All the things I loved doing with you...

Photos

All the things I loved doing with you...

Photos

I miss you saying and doing...

Photos

You taught me...

Photos

I wish you were here for...

Photos

You would have loved this...

Photos

If you were here today I would tell you this...

A letter to you

A letter to you

Photos

Stories people tell me about you...

Photos

All the things I remember about you now...

Drawings & Art

Drawings & Art

Drawings & Art

I love you to the moon and back
and more than all the stars in the sky

Big hugs from
www.harpermartin.com.au

www.ingramcontent.com/pod-product-compliance
Lightning Source LLC
Chambersburg PA
CBHW061225150426
42811CB00057BB/1301